MW00876420

How to Become a Professional Dancer

HowExpert with Elly Sarfert

For more tips related to this topic, visit HowExpert.com/dancer.

Recommended Resources

- HowExpert.com – Quick 'How To' Guides on All Topics from A to Z by Everyday Experts.
- HowExpert.com/free – Free HowExpert Email Newsletter.
- HowExpert.com/books – HowExpert Books
- HowExpert.com/courses – HowExpert Courses
- HowExpert.com/clothing – HowExpert Clothing
- HowExpert.com/membership – HowExpert Membership Site
- HowExpert.com/affiliates – HowExpert Affiliate Program
- HowExpert.com/writers – Write About Your #1 Passion/Knowledge/Expertise & Become a HowExpert Author.
- HowExpert.com/resources – Additional HowExpert Recommended Resources
- YouTube.com/HowExpert – Subscribe to HowExpert YouTube.
- Instagram.com/HowExpert – Follow HowExpert on Instagram.
- Facebook.com/HowExpert – Follow HowExpert on Facebook.

Table of Contents

Introduction

Becoming a professional dancer is a long and challenging road. It requires training, discipline, and perseverance. Professional dancers must be both physically and mentally skilled in order to perform to their best ability, and maintain their body while in season. A dance career offers work that keeps you in shape, allows you to be creative, and makes you money all at the same time! There are many avenues to becoming a professional dancer, but here we have compiled a list of steps that are generally taken to achieve such a prestigious position

Chapter 1: Start Your Training

The first step in becoming a professional dancer is to train. Dancers spend years perfecting their art. There are many different types of dance, and they all have their own discipline, technique, and vocabulary. Dancers must spend countless hours teaching their body to complete specific movements and positions. Professional dancers are physically strong. They must have both flexibility and stability. They must have strong feet and legs, and understand how to hold themselves in a proper way that is specific to dance. Proper dance technique is taught at local dance studios throughout the country.

Find a local dance studio that offers beginner lessons. It is never too late to learn a new skill; however, most dancers begin training from a very young age. It will take many years of training to build the muscle memory needed to perform at the highest level of dance.

When choosing a dance studio you should research both the credentials and the facility the business has to offer. Inquire what training the teachers at this studio have. Ask where they learned to dance, and what their background is. A dance teacher should have a vast background and knowledge of both dance technique, and the anatomy of the body. Often it is helpful if the teacher has their own performance experience, but it is not always necessary. What is most important is that the teacher understands the anatomy of the body, and can instruct the student on how to accomplish new skills without injury. Request a biography of each teacher, and research what schools they attended, or what companies they were a part of.

In the United States there are no requirements of accreditation for dance instructors, but a teacher who is a member of the Dance Educators of America association will have gone through educational classes about dance teaching. This higher education is a big positive when choosing an instructor. If you select a teacher who is a member of Dance Educators of America (DEA) you can be certain that your teacher is qualified. DEA offers continuing education classes, requires membership fees, and is a great network for a teacher to be a part of. To join the teacher must have at least four years of teaching experience, and have passed two of the entrance examinations in specific dance techniques. Ask students at the studio if they feel challenged and motivated by their teachers. Research if the studio has any alumni who are working professionally, or if they often send students to higher levels of education.

The studio should also have a facility that is safe for movement. Dance studios should have sprung floors, meaning the floor where you will be dancing has give and take, and will not cause joint pain. Marley floors are preferable, as they provide a surface ideal for turning and leaping. There should be mirrors along the walls for you to look at yourself and correct your alignment and positioning. The space should be clean, and large enough for jumps and progressions across the floor. You also may want to inquire about any extra equipment the studio has. Do they have state of the art tumbling mats for acrobatics classes? Do they provide therapeutic tools such as therabands, and foot stretchers? Do they have yoga mats for stretching classes? These sorts of amenities can be a clue as to the level of training that goes on at the business.

Ask how many students will be in each class. The smaller the student to teacher ratio the more hands-on instruction you will receive and the more space you will have to safely move. Inquire if private lessons are available, and how many classes a week a typical dancer takes. To become professional dancers need to be taking upwards of 25 hours of dance a week by the time they are in high school. Ballet technique should be a strong priority at the school, as it is the foundation of all styles of dance. Ask how many ballet classes are offered a week, and at what levels. You should go no more than two days without a ballet class throughout your training.

You should also choose your dance studio based on their options for growth. After you progress past beginner classes what sort of intermediate and advanced classes do they offer? Are there ample levels to progress through? Do they have any alumni who have gone on to attend conservatories or perform professionally? Do they offer a competition team? Many dancers choose to compete, as it adds incentive to perform, and allows for them to meet other dancers and teachers from outside of their own dance studios. If the studio does not compete, what other types of performance opportunities do they offer? Dancers learn from performing, and need the opportunity to become comfortable on stage and not just in the classroom. You should select a studio that will allow you to grow and mature as a dancer, and has a track-record of producing excellent talent.

List of factors to consider when selecting a studio:

Dance Teacher credentials

State of the Art facilities

Room to Grow and Progress through levels

Performance Opportunities offered

Alumni Accomplishments

Once you have selected a dance studio to attend you will begin classes. Ballet training is the foundation of all dance technique, and ballet classes are necessary for beginners and advanced students alike. In ballet class you will learn the positions of the body, and the fundamentals of dance. Ballet class uses French vocabulary to name the movements involved.

You will perform exercises at the ballet barre. The ballet barre is a wooden pole that extends horizontally on the wall at hip height. You hold onto the barre loosely as you perform technical exercises designed to increase turn-out, flexibility and strength. The Ballet barre exercises will slowly warm up the body and increase blood flow and muscle warmth. The class will then progress to the center, where you will complete different exercises.

After you have mastered the basics of ballet, you should branch out to other techniques of dance including modern, jazz, tap, hip-hop, and ballroom.

Each technique has its own vocabulary and movement style that will need to be mastered and practiced. You should build up your dance class schedule gradually. Advanced students often take four or five classes a day, and sometimes nearly 40 hours of dancing a week.

When attending your first dance class, there are many etiquette rules to consider. Always arrive early. Being on time is considered late in the dance world. Fifteen minutes is enough time to give yourself a gentle stretch and acclimate to your surroundings. Inquire about the studio's dress code, and adhere strictly to it. Most dance studios will require tights and a leotard for ballet, and tight fitting clothing for other types of dance. For ballet class women should wear their hair in a bun or French twist. Men typically wear black tights and a clean white t-shirt. In general your clothing should be solid colored, simple, and not too distracting for the teacher. No ripped tights or loose and baggy sweats. Some teachers will allow warm-up clothes to be worn, such as leg warmers, sweaters, or leggings over tights, but it is important to shed these layers by the time the barre portion of the class is over. Do not wear any jewelry that will fly off or injure you or others. At many studios a certain color scheme is required for each level. For example, younger dancers will wear pink leotards, middle-school aged dancers will wear light blue, and advanced dancers will wear black. Come prepared for whatever unique circumstances your particular school has.

When you arrive begin warming yourself up on your own. Come into class focused and ready to work. Many dancers use a foam roller or tennis ball to roll out their muscles before class. They also participate in light stretching and abdominal work. When the classroom is available, walk in and find a spot at the barre. If you are new to the class stand near the back where you can watch others and take after their example. There is no talking in a dance class, and respect must be paid to the teacher. As you progress through the class the teacher will call out corrections for the group as a whole, or specific students.

A "correction," is something the teacher tells you to fix about your dancing. A correction could be about your alignment, your technique, your expression, or your musicality. It is important to correct yourself right away. It is disrespectful to ignore corrections, and it will also not help you to improve. If another person in the class is given a correction, take the correction for yourself as well. When dancing in groups, always watch the other group on the side of the room. You can learn a great deal by observing your classmates and listening to their corrections.

Never talk while other dancers are dancing. When standing in the center for the adagio or allegro parts of the class, it is common practice that the least experienced dancers stand in the back of the classroom. You will be able to watch the more advanced dancers train in front of you, and learn from their example. If there is a musical accompanist, meaning someone playing live music for the class, never stand in front of them while waiting for your turn to dance. If you stand in front of the accompanist you are blocking their vision of the dancer and instructor, and impeding the class from progressing as it should. When the class is over be sure to thank both the accompanist and teacher. In different dance styles there are different customs of thanksgiving, but in ballet specifically a curtsy is acceptable.

Aside from dance classes, you should also cross-train as an aspiring professional. Dancers need to be versatile athletes, capable of both fast and slow movements. Pilates training can create a strong core and stream-lined physique. Yoga helps dancers to be centered and flexible. Weight training allows the dancer to be strong and powerful. All types of exercise are helpful. A strong and lean body is ideal for dancers.

Pilates in particular is often used to enhance dance training. Joseph Pilates created a system of moving that engages the core muscles, and allows for a slim and long physique. He originally created his reformer, a piece of equipment that uses springs to create resistance, for fallen soldiers in World War II. He then went on to work with the New York City Ballet, and Martha Graham the founder of modern dance.

Pilates uses a set progression of exercises, much like ballet, to work every muscle of the body. The Pilates system focuses on the stability of the pelvis and the strength of the abdominal core. By practicing Pilates you will train your body to be strong and flexible. Pilates also helps dancers to understand how to hold the pelvis correctly- a concept crucial to technically superior dancing. Pilates is a great way for dancers to cross train and enhance their performance.

In general when training there are a few basic goals all dancers should aim to accomplish. Having splits on either side all the way to the floor is a major necessity for dancers. Also stretching your middle split can increase turn out and flexibility. Dancers need a strong shoulder and back to complete technical arm and head movements. They also need a flexible spine, and ample mobility. Dancers often covet high arched feet, and strengthening your feet and ankles is incredibly important. There are many pieces of equipment you can buy to enhance your ankle strength and balance. Balance boards, therabands, tennis balls, foam rollers; the list of equipment that is helpful goes on. As you continue your training teachers and peers will help you to understand how to use all of these things to your advantage.

You will need to decide whether or not you want to compete. If you have chosen a studio that does attend dance competitions, your training will be drastically different than at a school that does not. Some teachers will argue that competing takes away the artistic integrity of dance, but there are many benefits to competing for growing dancers. Dance competitions are an opportunity to get an outsider's opinion on your personal technique and stage presence. At each dance competition there will be a handful of judges who will give corrections and critiques as they adjudicate you. All of these critiques will be available to you and your teacher to explore after the competition. Some competitions offer voiceover tapes, where the judges speak their corrections into a microphone as you dance. This can be a helpful tool for playing the corrections out loud as you complete the dance and hear them in real time.

Competitions also offer performance opportunities. Most studios will attend three to four regional competitions throughout the year, and one national competition in the summer. This allows for five different performance venues. If a child grows up performing in front of large audiences they will be more comfortable as an adult when auditioning and performing. It also raises the bar for training as dancers see what other students are accomplishing. Healthy competition is great for progression!

Many competitions also offer masterclasses from their judges in the mornings of competition days. These classes, often called convention classes, are mini intensives where dancers can learn from working professionals. Often competitions will offer scholarship awards to top-scoring competitors and allow their winners to attend their convention classes all year. Many dancers have used competitions as a platform for success. By winning many regional and national titles, they have gotten their name out into the industry.

The judges at well-known competitions are also the choreographers for some of the top shows in the industry, and if you have grown up performing in front of them they are likely to hire you when you come of age. Many dancers grow their social media presence through posting competition dances and wins. Some competitions even offer college scholarships to senior dancers, and have helped put many students through arts school. The dance competition world could be considered an entire industry in itself, and has helped many dancers to create a podium for success in their future dance careers.

Chapter 2: Attend a Summer Intensive

Once you have mastered the basics of dance, and have moved on to taking intermediate level classes, you should find a summer dance intensive to attend. Summer intensives are camps dancers attend to broaden their training and increase their skill in a finite amount of time. When choosing a summer intensive consider your ultimate goals.

Many Intensives are affiliated with dance companies, universities, or theaters. If your goal as a professional dancer is to someday perform with a specific company, it is a good idea to attend their summer intensive so that you can form a connection with their teachers, and learn more about their style. If you have a broad goal of being a ballet dancer, consider summer intensives based solely for ballet dancers. There are also many musical theater dance intensives, and modern dance intensives to choose from. Research online what the program is like, and be sure to inquire about your day to day schedule.

When choosing a summer intensive you should consider the same factors as choosing a home dance studio, but also keep in mind that this training should be specialized for your own personal goals. At these intensives you will meet people from outside your immediate circle, and these relationships may help you to gain future opportunities. Summer intensives also provide young dancers with constant training, without the interruption of school. Since school is out, you will be able to dance all day and concentrate solely on your craft. Think of Summer Dance intensives as a boot camp of sorts. Your body and your mind will change drastically. Absorb as much information as possible. Many dancers credit their dancing to great summer dance experiences.

Most well-known summer intensives will require an audition to attend. At this audition students will be asked to take class from the summer intensive's teachers, while being observed and adjudicated by administration. Do your best in the audition, and show them how you work. Most teachers want to see that you are focused and willing to apply corrections. You will be judged on body composition, ability to learn choreography quickly, and overall technique. The people judging these auditions know that you are not yet a professional, and they expect you to make mistakes. However, they will be judging how you overcome these mistakes, take corrections, and focus in class. They want students who are willing to learn and will improve over the summer.

Paying for Summer Intensives can be costly, but many programs offer merit and need-based scholarships. Inquire what the specific options are for your intensive, and ask if there will be a specific audition for scholarship recipients. If no scholarships are available, consider being sponsored by your local dance studio. At the American Dance Festival, students can have scholarships matched if their studio is willing to sponsor and support their attendance. Your studio wants you to be the best dancer you can be. Your success is their success!

When attending the Intensive, make sure to make the most of your time there! Some will be as short as one week, while others will last the entire summer. Quite often your schedule will go from dawn until dusk. Programs with showcases at the end will require dancers to have rehearsal in the evenings after a long day of classes. Intensives are grueling and demanding, but you will come out a much stronger dancer. Come prepared and ready to learn. It is important to fuel your body with high-quality food, and get plenty of rest and water during this process.

Teachers will expect you to be focused and ready for new information at all times. It is important to impress these teachers. Speaking with them outside of class can help you to formulate a bond that can be helpful later in your career. The dance industry is a small world, and connections are key when it comes to being accepted into colleges, or getting jobs. Professionals you work with as a student may later hire you if they remember you have an excellent work ethic.

Make sure when you arrive back at your home studio you continue to improve, and do not become stagnant. Often times dancers will go away to summer intensives and return with a remarkable amount of growth only to lose everything they learned. If you were challenged more at your summer program than you are at your home studio, take the initiative to keep that momentum going when you return home. Use what you learned to fuel your classes throughout the year.

Chapter 3: Apply to a well-known school for advanced Training

If after attending a summer intensive you feel you have improved vastly, and are now an advanced student, it may be time to apply to an advanced training program. Most professional dancers have trained at well-known and accredited schools where they were taught by the best in the business. Not only does advanced training make you the best dancer possible, it also allows you to network for the future. You teachers will be professionals who are involved with the industry, and your peers will be the future of dance. Your classmates may hire and fire you in the future, so it is important to be kind and courteous to everyone. In a small industry there is no room for burned bridges. This advanced training may come in the form of a ballet school, a performing arts high school, or a University.

The debate whether dancers need to seek higher education is a constant hot topic in the dance industry. University programs allow students to grow as performers, and study their art as an academic subject. For some, attending college is a necessary stepping stone towards a career. Others are ready straight out of high school to begin working. This is a personal choice. Training and readiness should be considered. The sub-industry you wish to be a part of should also be considered. Many modern companies, and Musical theater companies prefer their performers be a bit older and more mature, while ballet companies do not see University as a necessity.

This has changed recently however, as the trend leans more towards ballerinas also going to college. In the end the decision should be based on personal readiness.

If you do choose to attend a University, picking a program can be difficult. There are hundreds of schools all across the country that offer dance majors, but you will need to discern which programs will cultivate growth and give you the best opportunities. Some are conservatory based programs. In a conservatory program you will take many classes a day. You will take repertory classes, and learn about the art of dance. You will be trained to perform at a high technical proficiency, and much will be demanded of you. Non-conservatory programs tend to focus more on the academia of dance. These programs are great for those who want to be teachers, or start their own dance-related businesses.

As a dance major you will be required to take a certain number of credit hours per discipline. Some programs will require you to choose a specialty; jazz ballet modern etc. Others will ask you to be a versatile performer and train in all styles. Most likely you will be dancing daily, from 9 in the morning through evening rehearsals. You will also take academic classes that will enhance your understanding of dance in general, and the human body. Classes that are often required include; biology, kinesiology, art history, music fundamentals, dance history, and music theory.

In college you will need to choose a school with ample performance opportunities. Many schools bring in guest choreographers to set work on their students.

This is a great way to network for further opportunities in the dance world. These guest artists are often currently producing work, and if a strong bond is formed may hire you upon your graduation. Colleges typically treat their performances as professional shows, and allow for their students to learn what will be expected of them in the real world settings. College offers a time for exploration and growth as an artist, and human being. It is an excellent option for aspiring professionals.

The college audition process can be costly and grueling. Colleges often hold multiple auditions each year, where you will take multiple classes in different styles. At some schools where they are more focused on composition, you may be asked to come prepared to perform a self-choreographed solo. When choreographing this solo aim to show your own unique creative expression, while also showcasing technique and special skills. If you are applying to a musical theater school you will also need to be prepared with a monologue and song. Remember that just as in summer intensive auditions, schools are looking for potential and not perfection.

If you do not choose to attend a University, there are many other options for advanced training. There are public and private Performing Arts high schools throughout the country. Like a university, these schools allow students to focus on their art, while supplementing them with academic classes needed to understand their bodies and craft better. Often the day is spent dancing, with only a few hours designated to classroom time. Many of these schools are also boarding schools, so living arrangements are to be considered.

If you are an aspiring ballerina, most ballet companies have affiliated schools where they will groom dancers to be professionals in the future. Most of these programs will require an audition. The audition process will be similar to the summer intensive process, but perhaps slightly more demanding. Class will be given. Each hopeful will wear a number in bold letters safety pinned to their leotard. Teachers will be looking for an attention to detail and a willingness to learn.

Each school may have a style of performer they prefer. For example, Lines Ballet is known for its long legged dancers, while American Ballet Theater prefers a more petite aesthetic. You will most likely audition for many schools. Remember that while they are judging you at these auditions, this is also your time to judge them. In the event that you are accepted to multiple campuses, gauge your decision based on the audition class. If you very much enjoyed a class given at a specific school, or found the audition to be challenging and informative, this school may be the best choice for you!

Chapter 4: Focus On Your Own Personal Style and Sub-industry

Now that you have attended higher-education, it is time to get serious about finding a job. Branding yourself in this industry is important. There are so many different needs and niche's within entertainment, it can be a daunting task to find where you fit in. You need to decide what style of dance you will be pursuing professionally and what dance types you are most marketable in. There are ballet companies, modern companies, Broadway shows, regional theater, industrials, television, back-up dancing, theme parks, and cruise ships to name a few. All of these sub-industries have their own specific avenues. Setting goals and knowing where you want to end up will influence what steps you take towards employment.

Choosing a style to focus on can be hard, especially when dancers are taught to be as versatile as possible. Ask your teachers which dance styles they think you succeed in. If you have high-arched feet and beautiful turn out, you may be a natural at ballet. If you are a very stylized mover, and have an edgy modern look, you may be a great commercial dancer. If you prefer to explore movement and work with creative artists a modern company may be the right place for you.

Write down lists of your physical strengths, your mental strengths, and your work condition preferences. Use these lists to make the best decision. The type of dance you enjoy most, and the type of dance you are the most marketable in may be two very different things. Just because you enjoy a hip-hop class does not mean you are right for the movement. Ask trusted colleagues and friends what they believe your strengths are, and then begin to focus on those styles. In general when becoming a professional dancer you will either be joining a dance company, or you will be a free-land worker.

Ballet dancers have trained seriously in ballet their entire lives and have a vast knowledge of the specific technique and repertoire of ballet. Ballet dancers have high-arched feet, long and limber legs, excellent turn-out, and body control. Women are proficient on pointe, and men are able to lift and partner women. Ballet companies perform both classical and contemporary works. In a ballet company you will need to move up the ranks of hierarchy.

Modern dancers work in their bare feet and understand how to use contraction and release. In a classical modern company you will learn repertoire created by the great modern choreographers, as well as new works. More boutique contemporary companies are smaller, and focus more on post-modern work that is highly abstract and theatrical.

Jazz dancers can perform in musical theater, commercials, and industrial work. Women are typically proficient in character heels, and men wear street shoes or jazz shoes. Ballroom dancers know many styles of ballroom. They are flexible, able to perform complex patterns, and know their own specific technique. There are many other types of dance and niches, and many dancers are able to cross over between dance styles. However, it is important when you are first starting out to explore what you excel in, and go after that avenue head first.

The dance style you select may dictate whether you pursue life in a company, or as a free-lance performer. As a company member you will be a part of an organization that performs a full season of work. Casting for each production will come internally from within the company.

There are ranking systems of seniority within the company that you will need to climb through. Many companies will also have "second companies," or "apprenticeships," for newcomers. These positions are often either un-paid or compensated by stipend. However, by serving in these positions you will be able to train with the company, understudy roles, and prove your worth to the administration.

Above apprentices is the corps de ballet. The Corps is the bottom tier of hierarchy. These are the youngest and least experienced dancers, but they are full paid positions within the company. They are often used for ensemble work, and understudying soloists.

The next level of hierarchy is soloists, who perform lead roles on top of ensemble and feature parts. The highest position is a principal dancer. These dancers have been with the company for many years. They are the highest paid, and are first picks for lead roles and performances.

When joining a company you will most likely sign a contract. This contract may extend for only one season. This means each year you will have to prove yourself an important part of the company in order to renew your contract. Principals, however, may have multiple year contracts and more job security.

Free-lance workers have even less job security, but will perform in a plethora of styles and venues. Regional theater productions, tours, cruises and theme parks, and commercials all hire seasonally. This means you will be contracted for one show, and then will have to re-audition for the next show. Free-lance dancers bounce around from place to place. They are constantly auditioning, and marketing themselves. It is Important for freelancers to understand their brand and image, and know which parts are right for them. Although this life is less stable, it also offers to opportunity to travel and work in many different places.

Once you have chosen an avenue for your dance career it is important to relocate to a city that best fits your needs. New York City offers a wide range of dance, including boutique contemporary companies, modern companies, ballet companies, and of course Broadway. Los Angeles offers auditions and opportunities for dancers wishing to be in the television and film industry, as well as industrial work, video work, and some theater. Chicago has become a hotspot for modern and contemporary dance, while Miami is known for its ballroom and hard-hitting jazz. Other cities such as Nashville, Atlanta, and Pittsburgh have been growing in their dance industry, and offer some work for regional performers.

Research a city that best fits your standard of living, and your goals. Relocating is important so that you can begin to take class in the area and create relationships with other local professionals. If financing a move is an issue for you, talk to your home studio owners. They may be willing to sponsor you, or hire you to teach beginner students. Save up your money, and prepare to take the next big step towards your career in dance!

Chapter 5: Prepare Your Marketing Materials

Once you have relocated, you must begin marketing yourself. Dancers must be savvy in how they present themselves to the world. To become a well-known performer you should create a strong reputation, and put your best foot forward when walking in the audition door.

In today's day and age social media is a big part of creating a brand and image for one's self. As a dancer you are your own business, and you need to treat everything you put online as a direct reflection of that business. Foul language, negativity, and inappropriate posts can be found by casting directors and inhibit you from booking a job. However, it is important to have a positive social media presence! Many casting directors and producers will look up your personal accounts to get a feel for the style of performer you are, and how you interact with the world around you. Posting photos of your dancing, and videos of your own choreography are a great way to get noticed. Always keep captions positive and upbeat. Choreographers want to work with optimistic individuals who bring a great energy to the rehearsal room. Make sure photos are flattering and show off your skill. Update the world on work you are doing. Post different classes you attend or workshops you participate in so that potential employers can see that you are constantly engaging with the dance industry. Present yourself as a hard-working and polished professional. Gaining followers, and following other artists can expand your circle and keep you in the loop for upcoming events and performances.

Many dancers create their own personal websites. This is a particularly good idea for free-lance dancers as they constantly market themselves to new employers. On this website you can display your headshot, resume, dance reel, dance pictures, links to reviews of your performances, and any other materials that market you. There are professionals for hire that can help you create a unique template, or you can find an online service and use a pre-made template for a small fee. The website domain you choose may cost a yearly fee, but it is helpful to choose something simple and easy to remember. You can then write this address in emails and on your resume for casting directors to make a quick reference to all of your work in one place.

When attending an audition or submitting for a job, you will be attaching a headshot to your resume. A headshot is a photograph that shows your face directly, shot from the shoulders up. Headshots are important because they allow for directors and choreographers to remember who you are and keep a face with a name long after you have left the room. You headshot should be inviting, and professional. Investing in good quality headshots is a must in this industry. Do not take a picture on your personal camera and assume it will do. Hire a professional who understands what the photograph is for, and has experience working with other dance professionals. Color copy, 8x10 prints are industry standard.

You will need to make a judgement call for posing based upon the specific job you are submitting for. For example, if you are auditioning for a Disney show you will want a smiling and excited facial expression. If you are submitting for a serious play, a coy facial expression may be more appropriate. Neutral hair and makeup are required. The most important element is that this picture actually looks like you. If you have dyed your hair recently, this needs to be represented in your headshots. Altering the photo to make yourself look thinner or more "ideal," will only confuse directors. If you look nothing like your photo in person you may run into trouble. Re-touching photos is okay for small things like blemishes or shadows, but do not photo-shop defining characteristics like your nose or jaw-line. If men have facial hair in their headshot, they should also have it in the audition room. Choose a picture that depicts your truest self.

This picture gives the casting team a glimpse into who you are. Wear solid colored clothing that does not distract from your own face, and show personality in your smile!

Resumes will be required at all professional auditions. This is your space to inform the director what your credentials are. At the top you should list your name, email, hair color, eye color, height, weight, and any union or agency you belong to. Then you should proceed to explain performance experience. You can break this up into categories, such as theater, industrials, and television. List previous jobs three columns. The first column should name the show, the second column should list your role in this show, and the third column should list either the theater where the performance took place, or the name of the director.

Example:

Thoroughly Modern Millie	Millie	The Grand Theater, NC
The Producers	Ensemble	Dir: John Doe

Next you should list your education. Be sure to mention well known schools you have attended, and list a few teachers who would give strong recommendations for you if they were called to do so. List any special honors, such as competition wins or scholarships to summer intensives. This is the place where all of your hard work and training pays off! At the very bottom list "Special Skills." This is a place where you can inform the team of any sort of unique ability you may have. Show personality and a sense of humor. A few examples of special skills are; acrobatic skills, roller blading, working with animals, driving, tap dancing, and aerial work. If a choreographer happens to need someone who could skate board across the stage, and she sees on your resume you can skate board, you are a sure hire!

Your resume should be neat, easy to read, and centered. Have trusted mentors help you to edit. Make sure nothing is spelled wrong, or grammatically incorrect. Place a small photo of yourself in the top left or right corner. This way casting teams will not have to flip back and forth to remember who you are. Be concise, and place the most impressive elements at the top and center where they can be read in a quick skim.

When it comes to resume content, build your experience through internships, summer stocks, and workshops. While in school, or as an entry level performer, apply to work for top theaters as an intern. Many schools and professional theaters offer internship opportunities for young aspiring professionals. You will often be compensated through free dance classes, and perhaps performance opportunities.

The importance of networking in the dance world cannot be stressed enough. Continue to form relationships by boosting your experience. One example of a stellar internship to have on your resume is the American Dance Festival intern position. The American Dance Festival is a six week school operation that offers summer intensive style classes to dancers of all levels, and also houses many world-renowned companies at the Durham Performing Arts Complex. As an intern you will be tasked with a multitude of jobs. Some interns assist in school preparation, such as scheduling studios, and shuttling students. Others work behind the scenes of the nightly performances. Through this program many young interns have created working relationships with artistic directors and performers of some of the most relevant and acclaimed companies of the moment. You are also allowed to take a dance class a day, helping you to train and learn new skills as you network.

When you have completed your resume, you will need to attach it to your headshot. Have headshots printed in an 8x10 format. Then print the resume on quality paper, and staple it in all four corners so that the writing is facing away from the actual photograph. Then trim the edges using scissors or a paper cutter so that the resume paper and photograph paper fit. This is what you will hand to the audition monitor when you enter an audition. Casting teams like this format so they can easily flip back and forth between your face and your resume content. The staples are important so that the two pages can be separated easily if needed.

Chapter 6: Find, Prepare for, and Schedule Auditions

Now that you have built your own brand, and have a headshot and resume ready, it's time to audition! You will need to find these auditions yourself, and create your own schedule and agenda to attend as many as possible. Auditions are posted in many different online and in print publications.

Backstage Magazine, and backstage.com are two great resources for all types of performers including dancers. For a yearly or monthly fee you can gain membership to backstage to access the time and place for hundreds of auditions throughout the world. Production companies and theaters post upcoming auditions. On backstage.com you can use a filter to show auditions in your local area. You can also filter search results based on compensations, types of jobs, union contracts, and many other particulars. The site also allows for members to create profiles and contact potential employees directly. You will be able to upload your branding materials such as headshot resume and dance reel, and directly submit to casting directors and choreographers.

Playbill.com is another great resource for performers. Similar to Backstage, but not requiring a membership, Playbill lists upcoming auditions. Playbill also publishes articles about upcoming projects and industry happenings to keep you up to date in the dance and entertainment world.

A more grass-roots approach to finding auditions is to go to the studios that typically hold them. At studios such as Pearl, Broadway Dance Center, and NOLA studios, there will be postings of the day's auditions on bulletin boards in the hallways and elevators. Sometimes dancers will arrive at these studios with the intent of attending one audition, only to see a posting for a different audition and decide to attend that one instead.

Word of mouth is also a great way to hear about auditions and opportunities. When you are in dance class speaking with peers and teachers keep an ear out for upcoming projects they are participating in and inquire if there will be auditions held.

When you find a posting online for auditions there will be a "breakdown," of the job. The breakdown will list the roles they are currently casting, and the type needed for each role. For example, they may ask for "Female Dancers, between 5'2" and 5'6" tall, ballet technique and tap dancing a must!" This means that if you are in this height range and have both ballet technique and tap training you will be a good fit for the audition. If the breakdown says, "Male, under 6', Acrobatics and ballroom required," You probably shouldn't waste your time! Breakdowns can be helpful for dancers to understand what to be prepared for in the audition room in terms of style and attire. The posting should also list what the pay and accommodations will be like for the job. It should also list the start and end dates of the contract.

The most important information to pay attention to in an audition posting is who will be in the room. By "who is in the room," dancers mean who the choreographer and directors are, who the casting agent is, and who will be making the decisions about who is hired. Knowing the names and backgrounds of the people in the room making the big decisions can be extremely helpful to the dancers. Research what sort of dancers and styles each choreographer like to work with. If you have a connection with the director, make sure to highlight that person on your resume. Overall prepare for an audition with the same amount of research that you would any other job interview, and know who you are trying to impress.

Chapter 7: Attend Auditions! Go For Your Dream!

Now that you have found the auditions- it's time to prepare and go for it! Every audition is different and catered to the specific needs of the job, but there are a few elements that will always generally be the same.

You will most likely be given a number. If you are attending an open-call, meaning anyone is allowed to audition no matter union status or agent representation, there will probably be hundreds of candidates ready to perform and compete for the job. The casting director doesn't have the time to learn everyone's name, so numbering off allows them to remember who you are and take notes.

You will want to arrive early to get a lower number, and also make sure you are seen. Casting teams are allowed to cut the line, meaning they stop seeing dancers after a certain number have arrived. If you are too late you run the risk of not even making it in the room. Choreographers also tend to teach choreography more quickly as the day goes by. Learning the initial combo in the first group can give you an advantage of having more time to prepare, and be the first to impress the casting team. You will be given a number to pin to your outfit. Make sure the number is visible and won't be hidden or wrinkled while dancing. Middle of the chest or on your stomach are probably the best places for it. Bring your own safety pins in case they are not provided.

Auditioning is often a waiting game. Once you are given your number you will be ushered to the holding room. This is an empty studio where you are allowed to warm up, primp, and prepare. The holding room will be crowded. Come prepared with a water bottle to stay hydrated and light snacks to keep your blood sugar up. There will be very little room to warm-up, but light Pilates and stretching will help you remain ready for whatever choreography is asked of you.

No matter what type of job you are auditioning for, there will be "cuts" made throughout the process. You will start in large groups, and slowly dancers will be thanked for their time and asked to leave. Remain calm and focused. There will be multiple rounds and you will need stamina in order to make sure you are on top of your game for the entirety of the day. Auditions can be as short as two hours or last an entire day. Be flexible and prepared for anything. When you first enter the room, no matter the style or job you are auditioning for, walk directly to the front of the room and make yourself seen. Have a positive demeanor about you. Confidence and energy are contagious and casting teams want to work with people who seem ready and willing to work hard.

Musical Theater auditions are often held in New York City at one of a handful of studios throughout midtown. In order to get a spot in line you will need to arrive at the studios very early in the morning. There will be an unofficial list that dancers will have written on a sheet of paper. Sign the list and remember the number next to your name. Most casting directors will honor the list and use this order to see dancers. A small handful however, will not use this list so it is important to stay in the area and remain aware. There is a website forum called Audition Update where performers will post whether lists are being accepted, and what is going on in the audition. On any given day in New York 10 or 20 auditions may be happening, and performers often try to jump from one to the next to be seen by as many theaters as possible.

Every audition will have a monitor. The monitor is the person who will administer the audition, keep the performers informed of what will take place, and assist the casting team in lining up the candidates. The monitor will arrive about an hour before the posted start time of the audition. They will announce the proceedings for the day. Those on the list will be called in large groups to learn a "type" cut. A typing cut is a short dance combination that shows technique and personality quickly. Casting directors use this combination to judge the dancer swiftly on whether or not they will be able to perform at the level necessary, and also if they have the proper look for the show.

Musical Theater calls for type-specific casting, meaning you must look a certain way to portray the characters in the story. Often times you may be one of the best dancers in the room, but if you are not the exact height, weight, coloring etc. you cannot be hired. After the typing round the number of people left will be cut in half. If you are asked to stay you should feel proud, and know that there is something they see in you that they want to explore. You will then be brought into the studio to learn choreography in smaller groups. You will perform this 1 to 2 minute dance in groups of three or four, and more cuts will be made. If the show calls for multiple styles you may be asked to exemplify those skills; this could include tap dancing, acrobatics, ballet, partnering, or jazz. After the casting team has seen all they need to in terms of dancing, you may be asked to sing.

For some dancers singing is a terrifying part of auditioning. Although there are some jobs that require only dancing, many musical theater jobs require at least some basic understanding of music and singing. At an audition you will need to have sheet music with you to give to the accompanying pianist. Tape or staple the sheet music back to back so that it reads like a book and the pages can be easily turned by the pianist. Mark the music in pencil where you would like to begin and end. The director will ask for either a 16 or 32 measure cut.

Sing a song in the same genre as the show. For example, if you are auditioning for Rock of Ages sing a rock song, and if you are auditioning for Mary Poppins sing a classic Musical Theater song. Walk into the room and go directly to the pianist. Tap out the tempo you would like to sing at for them. Avoid snapping the beat as many pianists find this to be rude. Specify any other needs you have. For example, many dancers prefer the pianist to play their "bell-tone," or the note they start singing on, for reference before they begin. Then walk to the middle of the room. You will "slate," meaning you will state your name, what you will be singing, and which show or composer the music is from. Make eye contact with the pianist so they know you are ready and then begin.

When singing look directly over the seated casting team. Making direct eye contact can be uncomfortable for all parties involved. Perform the song as you would on stage, with large amounts of energy and commitment. When you are finished smile and thank them. This will probably be the end of the day. Remember that you will be hired inevitably for your dancing, and most directors simply want to see that you can carry a tune and are willing to speak or

Ballet and Contemporary company auditions have slightly different protocols. You will often need to apply to audition. Send your headshot and resume through email to the head of the company's casting department, along with attached materials showing your work. A Dance reel is a great way to grab their attention. This is a 3 minute video compilation of your best dancing. You can also send performance reviews and dance photos.

Ballet companies will often ask for a photo of your arabesque, and tendu in second so that they can assess your placement, turnout, and feet immediately. If they are interested they will contact you and invite you to come to their audition. The audition will run more like a standard ballet class. There will be cuts throughout as well, but not as many groups as a musical theater audition. You will need to be prepared for barre, center, adagio and allegro work. A pas de duex, meaning man and woman partnering, section may be required. Pointe work will be expected.

What you choose to wear to an audition can make or break your experience. The way you present yourself is the first impression you are giving the casting team, and also says a lot about how you carry yourself as a performer. No matter the genre of dance, you want to look polished and professional. No dirty, tattered, or loose fitting clothing. Choose clothes that flatter your body and make you look long and lean. For ballet auditions, tights and leotards are standard. Women should wear pink tights, with no holes, to make their legs look long and muscular. For men, long tights or leggings that are trim, and a tight fitting shirt are acceptable. Girls, pick a leotard that flatters your body shape and will stand out in a crowd.

Since casting directors do not know your name yet, they may use what you are wearing to remember your dancing. For example, they may say to each other, "That girl in the bright pink is fantastic!" or, "The man with the blue leggings is doing very well." A small skirt may be acceptable at some companies, but if you feel comfortable without it then it's good to go bare. Bring pointe shoes that are broken in but not too worn down. Modern companies may want a slightly less uniform look. Wear clothes that show your unique style, and will move well as you dance. Never wear something that will hinder your performance, such as sweat pants that are too loose, or a headband that will fall off.

For both ballet and modern, wearing your hair in a bun or French twist is appropriate. Remember to hairspray fly away hairs and make sure the style will be secure throughout your dancing. If you hair falls out in the middle of the audition this shows that you have not properly prepared yourself. For musical theater auditions there is much more freedom in dress.

Research the specific show you are auditioning for, and wear something appropriate for the style. For example, when auditioning for West Side Story, girls often wear skirts to move around as the Shark girls do in the iconic choreography. For A Chorus Line auditions you may want to wear tan tights and a bright leotard, and for Legally Blonde auditions you may want to wear a short skirt and tight sports bra. Dress for your body, in an exciting outfit that makes you feel confident.

In ballet company auditions ballet slippers and pointe shoes will be required. Modern and contemporary auditions will be conducted in bare feet. Musical theater will require jazz shoes, character heels, taps, and sometimes ballet slippers. The idea is to come prepared for anything and everything. For theater shows your hair may be down or up, but must look styled and polished. Men should have their hair combed and out of their face. Facial hair should be trimmed. Dress as though you are trying to impress on a first date.

If you perform to the company standards, and make it through the entire day of auditions, you may be asked to a "callback." A callback is an extension of the audition, held on a future date. Callbacks allow directors and casting teams to see more of the performers they have narrowed their choice down to. You may be given material to prepare and present at the callback.

It is important to wear the exact same thing you wore to the original audition, even if it the very next day. As we previously discussed, your outfit may be how the casting directors have distinguished you, and if they wrote down, "Love girl in turquoise," but you show up to the callback in yellow they may not remember who you are. The same principal can be applied to hair makeup and shoes. Go into callbacks with confidence and a willingness to impress.

Many performers find it easier to book work when they are represented by an agent. Agents hold open call auditions for dancers to come and showcase themselves. If the agent believes you are a valuable performer and that they could adequately represent you, they will contact you and have a contract written up. These auditions work similarly to open-calls. Wear whatever you think best represents who you are as a performer. Agents want a plethora of talent in a wide variety of styles.

If you do book an agent they will submit you to invited calls. An invited call is an audition specifically held for performers with certain representation. This means you may be able to be seen by casting directors you wouldn't have necessarily met on your own. An agent can be a great tool to dancers, especially after they have gotten a solid foundation of experience. The downside of agency representation is that you do pay them a percentage of all earnings, but contracts can be negotiated. Hopefully the amount of work they help you book outweighs this sacrifice.

Chapter 8: Build Connections, Never Stop Growing

Once you have booked your first job, you have your foot in the door. However, there is still much work to be done! Dancers will audition their entire lives. Each contract and role will be earned. Professional dancers are constantly networking and re-auditioning. Each performance and rehearsal process can either raise or lower you reputation in the industry. When arriving at your first professional job come ready to work hard and make new acquaintances. Having a reputation for good work ethic and a kind demeanor can help you get the next job, and the job after that. The industry is a small world and many choreographers will talk about dancers they have worked with to one another. Remember to never burn bridges, and always put your best foot forward. Actively seek out choreographers you have worked with previously. Inquire about new projects they have worked on and see if they are able to use you.

You also want to keep up your education. Professionals take class. They never stop training and maintaining their body composition and skill. When participating in a performance schedule it is key to maintain optimal physical health. Warming up, cooling down, icing, and rest are crucial to keep yourself in peak physical condition. Many professionals use chiropractic or athletic training services. This career is one of the most physically demanding in the world, and you must keep your tools sharp.

Professional workshops are offered at many schools and studios across the country. Much like summer intensives for aspiring pros, Professional workshops offer current working professionals an avenue to train, network, and learn from their peers. If you know that a choreographer will be casting a new show soon, research and find out where they are teaching workshops and classes. This is a great way to become a familiar face to them. When you get into the audition room they will remember your work ethic in class. Workshops are also a wonderful way for professionals to challenge themselves creatively. Often once we become professional we are performing the same show over and over. Taking classes outside of your rehearsals and performances allows you to master new choreography and refresh your ability to learn and adapt. The discipline that you acquired in your early training will serve you well as you progress through your career.

Dancers are some of the hardest working professionals in the industry. They must be savvy business men and women, polished athletes, and creative artists all in one. Becoming a professional dancer is a long and hard road, but the reward of getting paid to do something you love makes it all worth it in the end.

Recommended Resources

- HowExpert.com – Quick 'How To' Guides on All Topics from A to Z by Everyday Experts.
- HowExpert.com/free – Free HowExpert Email Newsletter.
- HowExpert.com/books – HowExpert Books
- HowExpert.com/courses – HowExpert Courses
- HowExpert.com/clothing – HowExpert Clothing
- HowExpert.com/membership – HowExpert Membership Site
- HowExpert.com/affiliates – HowExpert Affiliate Program
- HowExpert.com/writers – Write About Your #1 Passion/Knowledge/Expertise & Become a HowExpert Author.
- HowExpert.com/resources – Additional HowExpert Recommended Resources
- YouTube.com/HowExpert – Subscribe to HowExpert YouTube.
- Instagram.com/HowExpert – Follow HowExpert on Instagram.
- Facebook.com/HowExpert – Follow HowExpert on Facebook.

Made in the USA
Las Vegas, NV
09 September 2021

29911781R00026